WORLD CONFERENCE ON SCIENCE

WORLD CONFERENCE ON SCIENCE

Editor

Dr. DIGUMARTI BHASKARA RAO

M.Sc., M.A., M.A., M.Ed. Ph.D.

Secretary
Academy of Communication Culture
Education Science and Service
1-22-10 Srinivasa Nagar
Guntur—522006
Andhra Pradesh
India

DISCOVERY PUBLISHING HOUSE

New Delhi

First Published - 2001

Reprinted - 2014

ISBN: 978-81-7141-612-7

World Conference on Science

Published by:

DISCOVERY PUBLISHING HOUSE PVT. LTD.

4383/4B, Ansari Road, Darya Ganj

New Delhi-110 002 (India)

Phone: +91-11-23279245, 43596064-65

Fax: +91-11-23253475

E-mail: discoverypublishinghouse@gmail.com

sales@discoverypublishinggroup.com

web: www.discoverypublishinggroup.com

Printed at:

Infinity Imaging Systems

Delhi

Contents

Preface

The World Conference on Science for the Twenty-first Century: a New Commitment (26 June - 1 July 1999, Budapest, Hungary), convened by the United Nations Educational, Scientific and Cultural Organization (UNESCO) and the International Council for Science (ICSU), provided a rare opportunity to analyse where the natural sciences stand today and where they are heading, what their social impact has been and what society expects of them. The Conference established what efforts should be invested to make science advance in response to both social expectations and the challenges posed by human and social development. In other words, it negotiated a new 'social contract' for science as we enter the 21st century.

The build-up to Budapest was marked by a rich preparatory process involving wide consultation and the holding of many associated meetings providing input to the Conference.

Some 1800 delegates representing 155 countries, 28 intergovernmental organizations (IGOs) and more than 60 international scientific non-governmental organizations (NGOs) took part in the Conference itself, including 80 Ministers of Science and Technology, Research and Education or their equivalents.

The Conference discussed the intimate interrelationship between science and technology, and their role in socio-economic development and environment. What is most appropriate for developing countries? The conclusion endorsed by the Conference is that capacity-building is essential for endogenous development and that each country should develop scientific knowledge in the fields that are most suitable for meeting its own priorities.

The results of discussions in Budapest are embodied in the two principal documents adopted by the Conference:

- the *Declaration on Science and the Use of Scientific Knowledge*, which underscores the political commitment to the scientific endeavour and to finding solutions to problems at the interface between science and society;
- the *Science Agenda - Framework for Action*, which contains specific commitments and recommendations with regard to capacity-building in science and the use of science for sustainable development.

Subsequent to the Conference, both documents were endorsed by the governing bodies of ICSU and UNESCO. The present book contains these two texts, which chart the way for follow-up to the Conference by all partners and stakeholders in science, including the research community, government bodies, IGOs, NGOs and the industrial sector. An *Introductory Note to the Science Agenda* prepared by the Conference Secretariat is also included. In addition, a note on the last page of the book summarizes ICSU's position on the contribution traditional knowledge can make to science.

The Conference witnessed the launching of a number of initiatives designed to give fresh impetus to regional cooperation in science. It is essential now to maintain the momentum built up in Budapest, both at the international and national levels. The different stakeholders may locate at a glance the paragraphs in the *Science Agenda* of particular relevance to them by consulting the enclosed table outlining the Basis for Follow-up Activities.

Each partner will, of course, retain responsibility for its own follow-up initiatives to the World Conference on Science, but UNESCO will act as a clearing house for all activities, in co-operation with ICSU. For this purpose, all partners are urged to keep UNESCO abreast of their follow-up actions. In turn, UNESCO and ICSU will develop - together with relevant United Nations organizations and donor bodies - concrete initiatives oriented towards strengthening international cooperation in science.

The Conference was but one step in a global process which concerns us all, for we are all stakeholders in our own and in our children's future. We all have a moral obligation to past on to future generations a healthy environment and decent standard of living. Achieving this goal will call for resolute political will on the one hand and responsible scientific research and development on the other.

Representatives of government, representatives of civil society, representatives of the scientific community, I urge you to do what you can - in your area of responsibility - to make a difference.

M. Iaccarino

Maurizio Iaccarino
Secretary-General
World Conference on Science

Acknowledgments

The World Conference on Science provided a unique forum for a much needed debate between the scientific community and society. It addressed and involved national governments and institutions, educational and research establishments, members of the scientific community, the industrial sector, intergovernmental organizations and international scientific non-governmental organizations as well as the media and the general public.

The World Conference on Science has proved to be a milestone event in the march towards a social contract for science as we begin the 21st century. The governments, representatives of civil society and the scientific community will find in this book on the World Conference on Science a wealth of ideas, proposals and recommendations for constructive change.

The original documents presented in this book are meant for the benefit of people involved in science. I am thankful to the UNESCO for reproducing the principal documents concerned to the World Conference on Science.

D. B. Rao

1
Declaration on Science and the Use of Scientific Knowledge

PREAMBLE

1. We all live on the same planet and are part of the biosphere. We have come to recognize that we are in a situation of increasing interdependence, and that our future is intrinsically linked to the preservation of the global life-support systems and to the survival of all forms of life. The nations and the scientists of the world are called upon to acknowledge the urgency of using knowledge from all fields of science in a responsible manner to address human needs and aspirations without misusing this knowledge. We seek active collaboration across all the fields of scientific endeavour, that is the natural sciences such as the physical, earth and biological sciences, the biomedical and engineering sciences, and the social and human

sciences. While the *Framework for Action* emphasizes the promise and the dynamism of the natural sciences but also their potential adverse effects, and the need to understand their impact on and relations with society, the commitment to science, as well as the challenges and the responsibilities set out in this *Declaration*, pertain to all fields of the sciences. All cultures can contribute scientific knowledge of universal value. The sciences should be at the service of humanity as a whole, and should contribute to providing everyone with a deeper understanding of nature and society, a better quality of life and a sustainable and healthy environment for present and future generations.

2. Scientific knowledge has led to remarkable innovations that have been of great benefit to humankind. Life expectancy has increased strikingly, and cures have been discovered for many diseases. Agricultural output has risen significantly in many parts of the world to meet growing population needs. Technological developments and the use of new energy sources have created the opportunity to free humankind from arduous labour. They have also enabled the generation of an expanding and complex range of industrial products and processes. Technologies based on new methods of communication, information handling and computation have brought unprecedented opportunities and challenges for the scientific endeavour as well as for society at large. Steadily improving scientific knowledge on the origin, functions and evolution of the universe and

of life provides humankind with conceptual and practical approaches that profoundly influence its conduct and prospects.

4. In addition to their demonstrable benefits the applications of scientific advances and the development and expansion of human activity have also led to environmental degradation and technological disasters, and have contributed to social imbalance or exclusion. As one example, scientific progress has made it impossible to manufacture sophisticated weapons, including conventional weapons and weapons of mass destruction. There is now an opportunity to call for a reduction in the resources allocated to the development and manufacture of new weapons and to encourage the conversion, at least partially, of military production and research facilities to civilian use. The United Nations General Assembly has proclaimed the year 2000 as International Year for the Culture of Peace and the year 2001 as United Nations Year of Dialogue among Civilizations as steps towards a lasting peace; the scientific community, together with other sectors of society, can and should play an essential role in this process.

4. Today, whist unprecedented advances in the sciences are foreseen, there is a need for a vigorous and informed democratic debate on the production and use of scientific knowledge. The scientific community and decision-makers should seek the strengthening of public trust and support for science through such a debate. Greater interdisciplinary efforts, involving both natural and social sciences, are a

prerequisite for dealing with ethical, social, cultural, environmental, gender, economic and health issues. Enhancing the role of science for a more equitable, prosperous and sustainable world requires the long-term commitment of all stakeholders, public and private, through greater investment, the appropriate review of investment priorities, and the sharing of scientific knowledge.

5. Most of the benefits of science are unevenly distributed, as a result of structural asymmetries among countries, regions and social groups, and between the sexes. As scientific knowledge has become a crucial factor in the production of wealth, so its distribution has become more inequitable. What distinguishes the poor (be it people or countries) from the rich is not only that they have fewer assets, but also that they are largely excluded from the creation and the benefits of scientific knowledge.

6. We, participants in the World Conference on Science for the Twenty-first Century: a New Commitment, assembled in Budapest, Hungary, from 26 June to 1 July 1999 under the aegis of the United Nations Educational, Scientific and Cultural Organization (UNESCO) and the International Council for Science (ICSU):

Considering :

7. where the natural sciences stand today and where they are heading, what their social impact has been and what society expect from them,

8. that in the twenty-first century science must become a shared asset benefiting all peoples on a basis of solidarity, that science is a powerful resource for understanding natural and social phenomena, and that its role promises to be even greater in the future as the growing complexity of the relationship between society and the environment is better understood,

9. the ever-increasing need for scientific knowledge in public and private decision making, including notably the influential role to be played by science in the formulation of policy and regulatory decisions,

10. that access to scientific knowledge for peaceful purposes from a very early age is part of the right to education belonging to all men and women, and that science education is essential for human development, for creating endogenous scientific capacity and for having active and informed citizens,

11. that scientific research and its applications may yield significant returns towards economic growth and sustainable human development, including poverty alleviation, and that the future of humankind will become more dependent on the equitable production, distribution and use of knowledge than ever before,

12. that scientific research is a major driving force in the field of health and social care and that greater use of scientific knowledge would considerably improve human health,

13. the current process of globalization and the strategic role of scientific and technological knowledge within it,

14. the urgent need to reduce the gap between the developing and developed countries by improving scientific capacity and infrastructure in developing countries,

15. that the information and communication revolution offers new and more effective means of exchanging scientific knowledge and advancing education and research,

16. the importance for scientific research and education of full and open access to information and data belonging to the public domain,

17. the role played by the social sciences in the analysis of social transformations related to scientific and technological developments and the search for solutions to the problems generated in the process,

18. the recommendations of major conferences convened by the organizations of the United Nations system and others, and of the meeting associated with the World Conference on Science,

19. that scientific research and the use of scientific knowledge should respect human rights and the dignity of human beings, in accordance with the Universal Declaration of Human Rights and in the light of the Universal Declaration on the Human Genome and Human Rights,

20. that some applications of science can be detrimental to individuals and society, the environment and human health, possibly even threatening the continuing existence of the human species, and that

the contribution of science is indispensable to the cause of peace and development, and to global safety and security,

21. that scientists with other major actors have a special responsibility for seeking to avert applications of science which are ethically wrong or have an adverse impact,

22. the need to practise and apply the sciences in the line with appropriate ethical requirements developed on the basis of an enhanced public debate,

23. that the pursuit of science and the use of scientific knowledge should respect and maintain life in all its diversity, as well as the life-support systems of our planet,

24. that there is a historical imbalance in the participation of men and women in all science-related activities,

25. that there are barriers which have precluded the full participation of other groups, of both sexes, including disabled people, indigenous peoples and ethnic minorities, hereafter referred to as disadvantaged groups,

26. that traditional and local knowledge systems, as dynamic expressions of perceiving and understanding the world, can make, and historically have made, a valuable contribution to science and technology, and that there is a need to preserve, protect, research and promote this cultural heritage and empirical knowledge,

27. that a new relationship between science and society is necessary to cope with such pressing global problems

as poverty, environmental degradation, inadequate public health, and food and water security, in particular those associated with population growth,

28. the need for a strong commitment to science on the part of governments, civil society and the productive sector, as well as an equally strong commitment of scientists to the well-being of society,

Proclaim the following;

1. Science for knowledge; knowledge for progress

29. The inherent function of the scientific endeavour is to carry out a comprehensive and thorough inquiry into nature and society, leading to new knowledge. This new knowledge provides educational, cultural and intellectual enrichment and leads to technological advances and economic benefits. Promoting fundamental and problem-oriented research is essential for achieving endogenous development and progress.

30. Governments, through national science policies and in acting as catalysts to facilitate interaction and communication between stakeholders, should give recognition to the key role of scientific research in the acquisition of knowledge, in the training of scientists and in the education of the public. Scientific research funded by the private sector has become a crucial factor for socio-economic development, but this cannot exclude the need for publicly-funded research. Both sectors should work in close collaboration and in a complementary manner in the financing of scientific research for long-term goals.

2. Science for peace

31. The essence of scientific thinking is the ability to examine problems from different perspectives and seek explanations of natural and social phenomena, constantly submitted to critical analysis. Science thus relies on critical and free thinking, which is essential in a democratic world. The scientific community, sharing a long-standing tradition that transcends nations, religions and ethnicity, should promote, as stated in the Constitution of UNESCO, the 'intellectual and moral solidarity of mankind', which is the basis of a culture of peace. Worldwide cooperation among scientists makes a valuable and constructive contribution to global security and to the development of peaceful interactions between different nations, societies and cultures, and could give encouragement to further steps in disarmament, including nuclear disarmament.

32. Governments and society at large should be aware of the need to use natural and social sciences and technology as tools to address the root causes and impacts of conflict. Investment in scientific research which addresses them should be increased.

3. Science for development

33. Today, more than ever, science and its applications are indispensable for development. All levels of government and the private sector should provide enhanced support for building up an adequate and evenly distributed scientific and technological capacity through appropriate education and research

programmes as an indispensable foundation for economic, social cultural and environmentally sound development. This is particularly urgent for developing countries. Technological development requires a solid scientific basis and needs to be resolutely directed towards safe and clean production processes, greater efficiency in resource use and more environmentally friendly products. Science and technology should also be resolutely directed towards prospects for better employment, improving competitiveness and social justice. Investment in science and technology aimed both at these objectives and at a better understanding and safeguarding of the planet's natural resource base, biodiversity and life-support systems must be increased. The objective should be a move towards sustainable development strategies through the integration of economic, social, cultural and environmental dimensions.

34. Science education, in the broad sense, without discrimination and encompassing all levels and modalities, is a fundamental prerequisite for democracy and for ensuring sustainable development. In recent years, worldwide measures have been undertaken to promote basic education for all. It is essential that the fundamental role played by women in the application of scientific development to food production and health care be fully recognized, and efforts made to strengthen their understanding of scientific advances in these areas. It is on this platform that science education, communication and popularization need to be built. Special attention still needs to be given

to marginalized groups. It is more than ever necessary to develop and expand science literacy in all cultures and all sectors of society as well as reasoning ability and skills and an appreciation of ethical values, so as to improve public participation in decision- making related to the application of new knowledge. Progress in science makes the role of universities particularly important in the promotion and modernization of science teaching and its coordination at all levels of education. In all countries, and in particular the developing countries, there is a need to strengthen scientific research in higher education, including postgraduate programmes, taking into account national priorities.

35. The building of scientific capacity should be supported by regional and international cooperation, to ensure both equitable development and the spread and utilization of human creativity without discrimination of any kind against countries, groups or individuals. Cooperation between developed and developing countries should be carried out in conformity with the principles of full and open access to information, equity and mutual benefit. In all efforts of cooperation, diversity of traditions and cultures should be given due consideration. The developed world has a irresponsibility to enhance partnership activities in science with developing countries and countries in transition. Helping to create a critical mass of national research in the sciences through regional and international cooperation is especially important for small states and least developed countries. Scientific

structures, such as universities, are essential for personnel to be trained in their own country with a view to a subsequent career in that country. Through these and other efforts conditions conducive to reducing or reversing the brain drain should be created. However, no measures adopted should restrict the free circulation of scientists.

36. Progress in science requires various types of cooperation at and between the intergovernmental, governmental and non-governmental levels, such as: multilateral projects; research networks, including South-South networking; partnerships involving scientific communities of developed and developing countries to meet the needs of all countries and facilitate their progress; fellowships and grants and promotion of joint research; progress; programmes to facilitate the exchange of knowledge; the development of internationally recognized scientific research centres, particularly in developing countries; international agreements for the joint promotion, evaluation and funding of mega-projects and broad access to them; international panels for the scientific assessment of complex issues; and international arrangements for the promotion of postgraduate training, New initiatives are required for interdisciplinary collaboration. The international character of fundamental research should be strengthened by significantly increasing support for long-term research projects and for international collaborative projects, especially those of global interest. In this respect particular attention should be given to the need for continuity of support for research. Access to these facilities for scientists

from developing countries should be actively supported and open to all on the basis of scientific merit. The use of information and communication technology, particularly through networking, should be expanded as a means of promoting the free flow of knowledge. At the same time, care must be taken to ensure that the use of these technologies does not lead to a denial or restriction of the richness of the various cultures and means of expression.

37. For all countries to respond to the objectives set out in this Declaration, in parallel with international approaches, in the first place national strategies and institutional arrangements and financing systems need to be set up or revised to enhance the role of sciences in sustainable development within the new context. In particular they should include: a long term national policy on science to be developed together with the major public and private actors; support to science education and scientific research; the development of cooperation between R & D institutions, universities and industry as part of national innovation systems; the creation and maintenance of national institutions for risk assessment and management, vulnerability reduction, safety and health; and incentives for investment, research and innovation, Parliaments and governments should be invited to provide a legal, institutional and economic basis for enhancing scientific and technological capacity in the public and private sectors and facilitate their interaction. Science decision-making and priority setting should be made an integral part of overall development planning and the formulation of sustainable development strategies.

In this context, the recent initiative by the major G8 creditor countries to embark on the process of reducing the debt of certain developing countries will be conducive to a joint effort by the developing and developed countries towards establishing appropriate mechanisms for the funding of science in order to strengthen national and regional scientific and technical research systems.

38. Intellectual property rights need to be appropriately protected on a global basis, and access to data and information is essential for undertaking scientific work and for translating the results of scientific research into tangible benefits for society. Measures should be taken to enhance those relationships between the protection of intellectual property rights and the dissemination of scientific knowledge that are mutually supportive. There is a need to consider the scope, extent and application of intellectual property rights in relation to the equitable production, distribution and use of knowledge. There is also a need to further develop appropriate national legal frameworks to accommodate the specific requirements of developing countries and traditional knowledge and its sources and products, to ensure their recognition and adequate protection on the basis of the informed consent of the customary or traditional owners of this knowledge.

4. Science in society and science for society

39. The practice of scientific research and the use of knowledge from that research should always aim at

the welfare of humankind, including the reduction of poverty, be respectful of the dignity and rights of human beings, and of the global environment, and take fully into account our responsibility towards present and future generations. There should be a new commitment to these important principles by all parties concerned.

40. A free flow of information on all possible uses and consequences of new discoveries and newly developed technologies should be secured, so that ethical issues can be debated in an appropriate way. Each country should establish suitable measures to address the ethics of the practice of science and of the use of scientific knowledge and its applications. These should include due process procedures for dealing with dissent and dissenters in a fair and responsive manner. The World Commission on the Ethics of Scientific Knowledge and Technology of UNESCO could provide a means of interaction in this respect.

41. All scientists should commit themselves to high ethical standards, and a code of ethics based on relevant norms enshrined in international human rights instruments should be established for scientific professions. The social responsibility of scientists requires that they maintain high standards of scientific integrity and quality control, share their knowledge, communicate with the public and educate the younger generation. Political authorities should respect such action by scientists. Science curricula should include science ethics, as well as training in the history and philosophy of science and its cultural impact.

42. Equal access to science is not only a social and ethical requirement for human development, but also essential for realizing the full potential of scientific communities worldwide and for orienting scientific progress towards meeting the needs of humankind. The difficulties encountered by women, constituting over half of the world's population, in entering pursuing and advancing in a career in the sciences and in participating in decision-making in science and technology should be addressed urgently. There is an equally urgent need to address the difficulties face by disadvantaged groups which preclude their full and effective participation.

43. Governments and scientists of the world should address the complex problems of poor health and increasing inequalities in health between different countries and between different communities within the same country with the objective of achieving an enhanced, equitable standard of health and improved provision of quality health care for all. This should be undertaken through education, by using scientific and technological advances, by developing robust long-term partnerships between all stakeholders and by harnessing programmes to the task

44. We, participants in the World Conference on Science for the Twenty-first Century,: a New Commitment, commit ourselves to making every effort to promote dialogue between the scientific community and society, to remove all discrimination with respect to education for and the benefits of science, to act ethically and cooperatively within our own spheres of responsibility,

to strengthen scientific culture and its peaceful application throughout the world, and to promote the use of scientific knowledge for the well-being of populations and for sustainable peace and development, taking into account the social and ethical principles illustrated above.

45. We consider that the Conference document *Science Agenda - Framework for Action* gives practical expression to a new commitment to science, and can serve as a strategic guide for partnership within the United Nations system and between all stakeholders in the scientific endeavour in the years to come.

46. We therefore adopt this *Declaration on Science and the Use of Scientific Knowledge* and agree upon the *Science Agenda - Framework for Action* as a means of achieving the goals set forth in the Declaration, and call upon UNESCO and ICSU to submit both documents to the General Conference of UNESCO and to the General Assembly of ICSU. The United Nations General Assembly will also be seized of these documents. The purpose is to enable both UNESCO and ICSU to identify and implement follow-up action in their respective programmes, and to mobilize the support of all partners, particularly those in the United Nations system, in order to reinforce international coordination and cooperation in science.

2

Introductory Note to the Science Agenda—Framework for Action

The present document, prepared by the World Conference on Science Secretariat, was not presented for fomal approval but was aimed at facilitating the understanding of the draft Science Agenda - Framework for Action. *It is retained here for the same purpose.*

THE NEW CONTEXT

1. Several major factors have transformed, and will continue to affect, the relationships between science and society as they have developed in the second half of the century.

   (a) Scientific research is increasing our knowledge and ability to understand complex systems and processes in an ever-wider range of scales in space and time. The natural sciences are enjoying a highly creative phase stemming from breakthroughs and advances in various fields, from molecular biology and biochemistry, quantum physics and material science to the planetary sciences and astronomy. The emergence of new disciplines and of interactions among them, increasingly powerful computational tools, the rapid accumulation of scientific knowledge, and the need to bring together the natural and the social sciences in joint agendas, are having strong implications on scientific research and education.

(b) The conditions for the production and sharing of scientific knowledge are themselves changing as a consequence of the increasing intensity of communication, the growing interface between disciplines and tighter interactions between science and technology, universities and industry, laboratories and factories. Major economic and social implications are arising from the closer contacts between scientific discoveries and their application, technological know-how and commercial exploitation. Information and communication technologies are causing changes on all fronts as profound as those brought about when print first appeared.

(c) Linked to the changes occurring in science and technology are the globalization of trade and business, the growing role of transnational firms, and a reduction in the capacities of governments to regulate economic activity and its repercussions on society. Within a framework that is increasingly subject to transnational challenges and short-term requirements, competitive businesses are often those that can capture information flows and apply them quickly, rather than produce discoveries and inventions themselves.

(d) The end of the Cold War has resulted in a significant reorientation of investment in science and technology in some countries. For the most industrialized ones, resources dedicated to defence research during this period had represented a major part of public R & D expenditure. Unfortunately, in recent years, the percentage of GNP devoted to international cooperation, particularly with developing countries, has—with certain exceptions-stagnated or decreased. Taken together with economic difficulties, the result has been little or no growth worldwide in non-business funding for fundamental research, whist business R & D has declined in some sectors as a natural consequence of the stagnation of the global economy. At the same time, research programmes, especially large ones designed to address global problems, are subject to increasing costs.

(e) Growing inequalities on all fronts that contribute to new tensions and conflicts today beset the world. The patterns of disparities are now more complex and more contrasted. As one of many instances that illustrate this situation on a global scale, we recall that 20 per cent of humankind share 86 per cent of the total private consumption. Within and between countries the benefits of education, culture, health services and other factors of human and social well-being are ever more unequally distributed. On the whole, while the industrially more developed nations have built up a strong capacity for scientific research and technological innovation, other countries - the majority - have yet to solve basic needs of their populations, and the least developed countries are struggling for survival. The varying degrees to which countries and regions adapt to the scientific and technological changes threaten to further accentuate inequalities in access to and production of scientific knowledge and technical know-how.

(f) A further major factor is the multiplication of the environmental problems that weigh on the future of our planet. Beyond the phenomena of population growth and increasing urbanization, industrial, agricultural and transport activities are bringing about a major transformation of the global environment with serious consequences for human health and the productivity of ecosystems. Human action has even started to affect the functioning of global life support systems such as the climate system. The need to adopt the precautionary principle, initiate anticipatory research, take preventive action, and indeed make sustainability an essential ingredient in any model of development has become more evident at a time when societies, cultures, economies and environments are becoming increasingly interdependent.

(g) The need to take into account ethical consequences when discussing futrue directions of science has become more urgent over the last few years, requiring an open debate within the scientific community and in society at large. In this context, scientists themselves have started to play an active role in defining and accepting their ethical responsibilities. Public understanding and awareness of science are important factors in the establishment of appropriate ethical guidelines and procedures.

(h) A feature of our times is the emergence of organized sectors of society demanding participation in democratic debates and decision-making, as well as transparency on all public issues. Alongside traditional actors, such as trade unions and political parties, strong new groups are coming to the fore, including the communication media, citizen movements, and a variety of non-governmental organizations, such as associations of parliamentarians, industrial professions and entrepreneurs. Many of these are concerned with the environmental and other issues that the sciences are expected to address. Some reflect a lay disenchantment and disregard for science, and a fear of the unforeseen or unknown consequences of some of its applications. the confusion about who speaks for science amongst the many sectors, and whose science can be trusted, adds to this public mistrust.

(i) Women as a majority of the world population are claiming an increased role in all activities, particularly in science and technology. Important institutional and cultural barriers that prevent the progress of women in science education and research and their taking on responsibilities on a par with men, need still to be removed. Achieving a better gender balance in scientific activities, itself being a strong desideratum for reasons of equity, also implies that the approach, and even the content, of scientific advances may change to focus more on the needs and aspirations of humankind.

2. There is today an accumulation of discoveries, applications and know-how that constitute an unprecedented source of knowledge, information and power. Never have discoveries and innovations promised a greater increase in material progress than today, but neither has the productive- or destructive - capacity of humankind left unresolved so many uncertainties. The major challenge of the coming century lies in the ground between the power which humankind has at its disposal and the wisdom which it is capable of showing in using it.

3. Guided by the conviction that it is both urgent and possible to take up this challenge, the participants to the Conference are determined to concentrate efforts on the production and sharing of knowledge, know-

how and techniques to address the major problems ahead - whether local, regional or global. It is evident to everyone today, however, that it is not science alone that will solve the problems. A new relationship needs to be built between those who create and use scientific knowledge, those who support and finance it, and those concerned with its applications and impacts; such are the essence and the spirit of the new commitment.

4. In considering the practical expressions of this commitment, it must be recognized that the relationship between scientific research, education, technological innovation and practical benefits is much more diverse and complex today than in the past, and frequently involves many players other than researchers. The progress of science cannot be justified purely in terms of search for knowledge. In addition, it must be defended - and increasingly so, in view of budgetary restrictions - through its relevance and effectiveness in addressing the needs and expectations of our societies.

5. Democratic decision-making on scientific matters requires participation of all groups of society. It also needs consideration and respect for national diversity, within a spirit of solidarity and cooperation. If only one sector of the population or a single groups of nations has an active role in science and its applications, disequilibria are likely to occur, and the gaps and disparities tend to increase. Therefore, in defining and carrying out the multilateral commitment to science it is not only important that each and every country be able to make its own informed and articulate

contribution, but also that all actors - the public, the media, scientists, educators, industrialists, politicians and decision-makers—be involved in the process.

THE NEW COMMITMENT

6. In the process leading to the World Conference on Science and to the drafting of the *Declaration on Science and the Use of Scientific Knowledge and the Science Agenda Framework for Action*, numerous reflections and enlightening debates have taken place. Among the wide variety of concerns and proposals expressed, there are clear signals of convergence with regard to some central issues. These are listed here as general guidelines to facilitate the identification of the new commitment.

   (a) Need for drastic changes of attitude and approach to problems of development, especially to their social, human and environmental dimension. The sciences must be put to work for sustainable peace and development in a progressively responsive and democratic framework; scientists, as all other stakeholders, must correspondingly recognize their ethical, social and political responsibilities.

   (b) Need to improve, strengthen and diversify science education, formal and non-formal, at all levels and for all sectors, and to integrate science into the general culture, emphasizing its contribution to the formation of open and critical thinking as well as to the improvement of people's ability to meet the challenges of modern society. Any discriminatory barrier operating against equitable participation in science must be removed, and positive efforts are needed to fully integrate women into the sciences.

(c) Need to strengthen the national S & T base, refurbishing national science policies, increasing scientific personnel and ensuring a stable and supportive research context, especially in areas of local and global relevance. In developing countries increased funding for S & T is needed, taking into account local capacities and priorities, and this funding should be augmented by similar commitments from developed partners.

(d) Need to break traditional barriers between the natural and the social sciences and to adopt interdisciplinarity as a common practice. Moreover, since the processes underlying present global problems and challenges need the concurrence of all scientific disciplines, it is imperative to attain a proper balance in their support.

(e) Need to open scientific matters to public debate and democratic participation, so as to arrive at consensus and concerted action. The scientific community is expected to open itself to a permanent dialogue with society. A dialogue with other forms of knowledge and expressions of culture is particularly relevant.

(f) Need to reinforce and broaden scientific cooperation, regional and international through networking and institutional arrangements with IGOs, NGOs, research and education centres. In this regard, the programmes of UNESCO and ICSU must be strengthened, in particular through cooperation between them and with other United Nations bodies. It is a challenge to improve the coordination of the various efforts of these partners, respecting their different roles and stimulating synergy between them.

BASIS FOR ACTION

The following text takes up all sections of the draft *Science Agenda - Framework for Action* and attempts to provide the general ideas behind the guidelines for action listed therein.

1. Science for knowledge; knowledge for progress

Role of fundamental research

7. The sciences are expected to continue to fulfil their intrinsic assignment which is the acquisition of knowledge and understanding, benefiting from the creativity of scientists around the world. This is the central argument for continuing to carry out fundamental research and education in all disciplines of the sciences.

8. Public authorities, private companies, universities, research laboratories and institutes each have their own dynamics and domains of action. In being associated with all such different partners, scientific research must cope with the underlying diversity

of contexts and adopt a coherent agenda, establishing a balance between immediate and long-term objectives.

9. In designing international policies and programmes for science, the multiplicity of conditions for scientific research, of perceptions of science, and also of problems, needs and possibilities to apply scientific knowledge be borne in mind. International science is ideally built upon the plurality and diversity of contributions that all nations can make to the scientific endeavour, in regard to their own capacities, needs and interests.

The public and private sectors

10. Fundamental research requires sustained public support, as it represents an off-market' publicasset with uncertain short-term profitability. The returns and applications deriving from it provide, in turn, new irrigation for the entire research system, while at the same time contributing to the solution of specific problems and the development of technological competences.

11. New funding mechanisms must be sought for science, taking into account the present context. In most industrialized countries private investment in S & T research surpasses that financed by the public sector, and a number of public institutions have been or are being privatized. Agencies awarding grants tend to give preference to research with short-term goals, and accountability of results is increasingly based on technological applications and patents rather than on basic knowledge acquisition. In the majority of

developing countries, on the other hand, most of scientific research is publicly financed. Even in those countries that have managed to build up a critical mass of scientists, the private sector gives preference to research with short-term goals or does not invest in research at all; the scientific system is weakly linked to the productive system and local industry does not benefit from the opportunities created by science; as a result, S & T contributes little to the creation of national wealth in these countries.

Sharing scientific information and knowledge

12. The new communication and information technologies have become an important factor of change, giving rise to new directions, methodologies and scenarios for scientific work and new ways of producing, accessing and using information. The growing impact and potential of the new technologies make it necessary for scientists and institutions to adapt themselves in order to fully benefit from the advantages they can bring. In this regard it is essential that they be developed and used to provide equal opportunities for scientists in different regions of the world, to facilitate the wide distribution and access of information, and to promote a truly international scientific dialogue. Computing and information systems that are reflective of the diverse cultures, languages, technical resources, habits and needs of people around the world, need to be designed.

13. True and comprehensive sharing of scientific knowledge cannot be accomplished by electronic

means alone. Regional and international networks for research and training, partnerships involving communities of developed and developing countries, and specific programmes for the exchange and transfer of scientific knowledge and skills, have proved to be important mechanisms and should be fostered and implemented more widely.

2. Science for peace and development

Science for basic human needs

14. Food, water, shelter, access to health care, social security and education are cornerstones of human well-being. Poverty and dependence affecting a number of countries can only be escaped through social and economic transformation and political determination, a comprehensive and upgraded education system, and the appropriate development and use of science and technology. Scientific knowledge needs to be applied to find ways of reducing the imbalance, injustice and lack of resources that particularly affect the marginalized sectors of society and the poorer countries in the world.

15. Science is today a currency in the hierarchy of nations. Developing countries need to enhance S & T capacities in areas that are relevant to the problems of their own populations and to their national development. It should not be overlooked, however, that these countries present a very mixed profile, some being in various ways closer to the industrialized world than to their fellow countries. It is essential that each country has

the capacity and takes on the responsibility to define its priorities and areas of relevance and how to address them.

16. It is against this background that a case for supporting S & T in developing countries is made. Such an effort will benefit these countries in solving their actual problems and achieving more healthy and sustained development. In essence, it will be of global benefit, since there are more than 120 developing countries, comprising three fourths of the global population. As long as these countries are not effectively involved in science, can we talk of world science?

17. There is need for urgency here. Comprehensive, far-reaching and lasting development is a universal challenge and is not restricted to a particular group of countries. It requires coherent, plural, multifaceted action, to which the international community has much to contribute.

Science, environment and sustainable development

18. One of the greatest challenges facing the world community in the next century will be the attainment of sustainable development, calling for balanced interrelated policies aimed at economic growth, poverty reduction, human well-being, social equity and the protection of the Earth's resources, commons and life-support systems. It is increasingly perceived that sustainable management and use of resources and sustainable production and consumption patterns in general, are the only pathways to meeting developmental and environmental needs of present

and future generations. We must enhance and harness our scientific capabilities to develop sustainably.

19. Taking into account the 'programme for the Further Implementation of Agenda 21' adopted by the United Nations General Assembly in 1997, the guidelines for action provided in the *Agenda* are expected to address the following key objectives: to strengthen capacity and capability in science for sustainable development, with particular emphasis on the needs of developing countries; to reduce scientific uncertainty and improve the long-term prediction capacity for the prudent management of environment-development interactions; to foster international scientific cooperation and the transfer and sharing of scientific knowledge; to bride the gap between science, the productive sectors, decision-makers and major groups in order to broaden and strengthen the application of science.

Science and technology

20. Science, technology and engineering are among the principal drives of industrial and economic development. The difference in abilities of countries to exploit S & T through the process of innovation contributes to an ever-increasing extent to differences in economic performance and to the widening income gap between industrialized and developing countries.

21. Innovation in all sectors is increasingly characterized by bidirectional feedback between the basic research system, and technology development and diffusion. This is changing the requirements for successful

technology transfer and upgrading of innovation capabilities in the developing countries, with implications for domestic policies and international cooperation. One of their main priorities must now be to promote the development of national scientific and technological infrastructures and of the corresponding human resoruces.

Science education

22. There is an urgent need to renew, expand and diversify basic science education for all, with emphasis on scientific and technological knowledge and skills needed to participate meaningfully in the society of the future. The rapid advancement of scientific knowledge means that the established education system cannot alone cope with the changing needs of the population at the various levels; increasingly, formal education must be complemented through non-formal channels. The communication media and technologies can play an important role in this regard. On a broader scale, an increasingly scientifically oriented society needs science popularization in its widest sense, to promote an improved understanding of science and adequately orient public perceptions and attitudes about science and its applications.

23. It is today widely recognized that without adequate higher S & T education and research institutions providing a critical mass of skilled scientists, no country can ensure genuine development. It is further agreed that action at national level should aim to tighten the links between higher education and research

institutions, taking into account that education and research are closely related elements in the establishment of knowledge.

Science for peace and conflict resolution

24. There can be no lasting peace as long as essential problems of development are not properly attended to; there can be no proper development as long as the culture and the practice of peace are not universally adopted. Were science always geared towards peaceful purposes, it certainly would make a greater contribution to the well-being of humankind.

25. Constructing the defences of peace in the minds of individuals, as recommended in the Preamble of UNESCO's Constitution, implies grasping the tools of scientific knowledge to reveal, understand and at the same time prevent the root causes of conflict. This field of research requires the concerted effort of a large number of scientific disciplines, involving as it does issues such as social inequality, poverty, food provision, justice and democracy, education for all, health care and environmental degradation. In other words, it involves every aspect of economic, social or political life that engenders violence.

26. The contribution to the construction of the defences of peace entils a great responsibility for all professionals active in science and technology. The principles of universality, freedom and critical thinking that are dear to science, constitute a common bond for a constructive dialogue between parts in conflict and serve to fight intolerance and ideological and social

barriers. Scientists have demonstrated the role that they can play in addressing conflicts and preparing peaceful agreements; this role must continue, with the support of governments and independent institutions.

Science and policy

27. Each country needs to have the capacity to design and implement its own science policy with responsibility within the global context, and to confront the dilemmas of priorities and competition for resources from the particular phase of economic development and industrialization in which it finds itself. A balanced development of a science base suitable for the country's needs requires an elaborate infrastructure and a stable institutional support, as well as the existence of an appropriate legal and regulatory framework. Regional and international networking and cooperation can facilitate the exchange of national experiences and the design of more coherent science policies. Requiring special attention are the legal issues and regulations guiding international research and development in strategic areas such as information and communication technologies, biodiversity and biotechnology Cooperation among international organizations is needed, to improve the measurement and understanding of intangible assets and recognition of thier importance and to protect the output of intangible investments in areas such as intellectual property rights. An internationally accepted framework should provide for the protection of intellectual property rights, recognizing the provisions in existing frameowrks that allow for different approaches.

28. In view of the increasing complexity of decision-making in the contemporary world, scientists should be more proactice in their contribution to national policy-making. The role of science in society and governance has never been more important. Science has an overriding responsibility to help societies make a transition to a dynamically stable and sustainable ecological and economic system. In this transition, an alliance between modern technical science and the holistic wisdom from traditional societies and philosophers from all cultures can be very important.

3. Science in society and science for society

Social requirements and human dignity

29. Science should be at the service of humanity as a whole, and contribute to improving the quality of life for every member of present and future generations. Those fields that promise to address issues of social interest need therefore to be high on the agenda. When dealing with science-society benefits, long-term vision in scientific planning is necessary, provided that intermediate objectives are defined so that appropriate evaluation can be undertaken. Different individuals, sectors or groups can have widely varying needs and requirements, according to parameters such as age, education, health, professional training, working place, living place, economic status, gender and cultural background. Identifying these diverse needs, and finding possible ways to address and fulfil them, require the concerted effort of scientists from different disciplines. The new reciprocal commitment between science and society will require not only that the

scientific community take account of these challenges, but also that the cooperation mechanisms be resolute in promoting a strategy to meet them.

30. The scientific community, governments, and all relevant institutions are urged to commit themselves to unrestricted respect for social and human dignity. In compliance with an essential social and moral duty, scientists should always work for the democratic principles of dignity, equality and respect of individuals and against ignorance, prejudice and the exploitation of human beings.

Ethical issues

31. The new discoveries and applications of science, while raising enormous hopes and expectations, also give rise to a variety of ethical problems; scientists, therefore, can no longer overlook the ethical implications of scientific work. Ethics is a subject for permanent debate, choices and commitments - at both the individual and the social level- that transcends juridical prescriptions and adapts itself to a diversity of evolving situations.

32. The full and free exercise of science, with its own values, should not be seen to conflict with the recognition of spiritual, cultural, philosophical and religious values, an open dialogue needs to be maitnained with these value systems to facilitate mutual understanding. For the development of an all-encompassing debate on ethics in science, and a possibly ensuing code of universal values, it is necessary to recognize the many ethical frameworks in the civilizations around the world.

Widening participation in science

33. All human beings have the right to particpate in the scientific enterprise. Equity in entering and pursuing a career in science is one of the social and ethical requirements of human development; there should be no discrimination in science, against any sector or individual. The increasing participation or involvement of all sectors of society in the scientific enterprise entails a systemic revision of science; it is clear that the decision-making and normative mechanisms of the institution of science are inevitably affected. In particular, any kind of central monitoring, whether political, ethical or economic, needs to take into account the increasingly diverse actors entering into the social tissue of science.

34. Women's particpation in the planning, orientation, and assessment of scientific research and education activities needs urgently to be increased, in order to benefit from their perspective on science and their contribution to it; only in this way can maximum use be made of the intellectural potential of humankind as a whole and the optimal contribution to human and social well-being ensured.

Modern science and other systems of knowledge

35. Modern science does not constitute the only form of knowlege, and closer links need to be established between this and other forms, systems and approaches to knowledge, for their mutual enrichment and benefit. A constructive intercultural debate is in order, to help find ways of better linking modern science to the broader knowledge heritage of humankind.

36. Traditional societies, many of them with strong cultural roots, have nurtured and refined systems of knowledge of their own, relating to such diverse domains as astronomy, meteorology, geology, ecology, botany, agriculture, physiology, psychology and health. Such knowledge systems represent an enormous wealth. Not only do they barbour information as yet unknown to modern sicence, but they are also expressions of other ways of living in the world, other relationships between society and nature, and other approaches to the acquisition and construction of knowlege. Special action must be taken to conserve and cultivate this fragile and diverse world heritage in the face of globalization and the growing dominance of a single view of the natural world as espoused by science. A closer linkage between science and other knowledge systems is expected to bring important advantages to both sides.

ANNEX: LIST OF RELATED CONFERENCES

The Declaration on Science and the Use of Scientific Knowledge and the *Science Agenda -Framework for Action* have taken into account the decisions, recommendations and reports of a number of recent major intergovernmental or non-governmental conferences, listed below, as well as the reports of associated meetings organized within the framework of the World Conference on Science.

- Recommendation on Status of the Scientific Researchers, adopted by the UNESCO General Conference, Paris, 1974.
- Vienna Programme of Action on Science and Technology for Development (UNCSTD), UN, New York, 1979.

- ICSU/ICASE/UNESCO International Conference on Science Education, Bangalore, 1985
- ICSU Statement on Freedom in the Conduct of Science, Paris, 1989.
- World Conference on Education for All: Meeting Baasic Learning Needs (Final Report), Jomtien, 1990.
- WMO/UNEP/UNESCO/ICSU Second world Climate Conference, Geneva, 1990
- Statement of the International Conference on an Agenda of Science for Environment and Development into the 21st Century (ASCEND 21), Vienna, 1991.
- Agenda 21 of the United Nations Conference on Environment and Development, Rio de Janeiro, 1992.
- Conference on Academic Freedom and University Autonomy, Sinaia, 1992.
- ICSU Statement on Gene Patenting, Paris, 1992.
- World Conference on Human Rights, Vienna, 1993.
- Report of the Global conference on the Sustainable Development of Small Island Developing States, Bridegetown, Barbados, 1994.
- Ageda for Development adopted by the Group of 77 in New York, 18 April 1995.
- World Summit for Social Development, Copenhagen, Denmark, 1995.
- Report of the Gender Working Group on Gender Implications of Science and Technology for the Benefit of Developing Countries of the United Nations Commission on Science and Technology 1995.

- Fourth World Conference on Women, Beijing, 1995.
- International Congress on Education and Informatics, Moscow, 1996
- ICSU Statement on Animal Research, Paris, 1996.
- World Food Summit, Rome, 1996.
- Programme for the further Implementation of Agenda 21, UN General Assembly, New York 1997.
- World Congress on Higher Education and Human Resources Development for the Twenty-first Century, Manila, 1997.
- Universal Declartion on the Human Genome and Human Rights, adopted by the UNESCO General Conference, Paris, 1997.
- World Declaration on Higher Education for the Twenty-First Century: Vision and Action. UNESCO, Paris, 1998.
- Framework for Priority Action for Change and Development of Higher Education, UNESCO, Paris, 1998.

3

Science Agenda - Framework For Action

PREAMBLE

1. We, participants in the World Conference on Science for the Twenty-first Century: a New Commitment, assembled in Budapest, Hungary, from 26 June to 1 July 1999 under the aegis of the United Nations Educational, Scientific and Cultural Organization (UNESCO) and the International Council for Science (ICSU), State the following:

2. Advancing the objectives of international peace and the common welfare of humankind is one of the highest and most noble goals of our societies. The creation of UNESCO and of ICSU, more than half a centruy ago, was a symbol of the international determination to advance these objectives through scientific, educational and cultural relations among the peoles of the world.

3. The above objectives are as valid now as they were 50 years ago. However, while the means of achieving them have developed considerably over this half-centruy through scientific and technological progress,

so have the means of threatening and compromising them. In the meantime, the political, economic, social, cultural and environmental context has also changed profoundly, and the role of the sciences (natural sciences such as physical, earth and biological sciences, biomedical and engineering sciences, social and human sciences) in this changed context needs to be collectively defined and pursued: hence the grounds for a new commitment.

Having adopted the *Declaration on Science and the Use of Scientific Knowledge,* and inspired by the Introductory note to the *Science Agenda - Framework for Action,*

4. We agree, by common consent, to the present *Science Agenda-Framework for Action,* as guidelines and instruments for action to achieve the goals proclaimed in the *Declaration.*

5. We consider that the guidelines for action formulated hereafter provide a framework for dealing with the problems, challenges and opportunities confronting scientific research and for the furthering of existing and new partnerships, both national and international, between all actors in the scientific endeavour. Such research efforts and partnerships must be consistent with the needs, aspirations and values of humankind and respect for nature and future generations, in the pursuit of lasting peace, equity and sustainable development.

1. Science for knowledge; knowledge for progress

6. We commit ourselves to the advancement of knowledge. We want this knowledge to be at the

service of humanity as a whole, and to produce a better quality of life for present and future generations.

Role of fundamental research

7. Each country should aim at having high-quality scientific institutions capable of providing research and training facilities in areas of specific interest. In those cases where countries are unable to create such institutions, the necessary support should be granted by the international community, through partnership and cooperation.

8. The conduct of scientific research should be supported by an appropriate legal framework at the national and international level. Freedom of opinion and protection of intellectual rights are particularly important in this respect.

9. Research groups and institutions and relevant non-governmental organizations should strengthen their regional and international cooperation activities, with a view to: facilitating scientific training; sharing expensive facilities; promoting the dissemination of scientific information; exchanging scientific knowledge and data, notably between developed and developing countries; and jointly addressing problems of global concern.

10. Universities should ensure that programmes in all fields of science focus on both education and research and the synergies between them and introduce research as part of science education. Communication skills and exposure to social sciences should also be a part of the education of scientists.

11. In the new context of increased globalization and international networking the universities are faced not only with new opportunities but also with challenges. For example, universities play an increasingly important role in the innovation system. Universities are responsible for educating a highly skilled workforce for the future and equipping their students with the capabilities needed to deal with global issues. They should also be flexible and regularly update their knowledge. Universities in developed and developing countries should intensify their cooperation, for example through twinning arrangements. UNESCO could act as a clearing house and facilitator.
12. Donor countries and agencies of the United Nations system are urged to foster cooperation in order to improve the quality and efficiency of their support to research in developing countries. Their joint effort should be focused on strengthening national research systems, taking into account national priorities and science policies.
13. Professional organizations of scientists, such as national and international academies, scientific unions and learned societies, have an important role to play in the promotion of research, for which they should be given wide recognition and corresponding public support. Such organizations should be encouraged to further international collaboration on questions of universal concern. They should also be encouraged to be the advocates of the freedom of scientists to express their opinions.

The public and private sectors

14. Through participatory mechanisms involving all relevant sectors and stakeholders, governments should identify the needs of the nation and give priority to support for the public research needed to achieve progress in the various fields, ensuring stable funding for the purpose. Parliaments should adopt corresponding measures and levels of budget appropriation.

15. Governments and the private sector should achieve an adequate balance between the various mechanisms for funding scientific research, and new funding possibilities should be explored or promoted through appropriate regulation and incentive schemes, with public-private partnerships based on flexible schemes, and governments guaranteeing the accessibility of generated knowledge.

16. There should be close dialogue between donors and recipients of S & T funding Universities, research institutes and industry should develop closer cooperation; financing of S & T projects should be promoted as a means of advancing knoweldge and strengthening science-based industry.

Sharing scientific information and knowledge

17. Scientists, research institutions and learned scientific societieis and other relevant non-governmental organizations should commit themselves to increased international collaboration, including the exchange of knowlege and expertise. Initiatives to facilitate access

to scientific information sources by scientists and institutions in the developing countries should be especially encouraged and supported. Initiatives to fully incorporate women scientists and other disadvantaged groups from the South and North into scientific networks should be implemented. In this context efforts should be made to ensure that results of publicly- funded research will be made accessible.

18. Countries that have the necessary expertise should promote the sharing and transfer of knowledge, in particular through support to specific programmes set up for the training of scientists worldwide.

19. The publication and wider dissemination of the results of scientific research carried out in the developing countreis should be facilitated, with the support of developed countries, through training, the exchange of information and the development of bibliographic services and information systems better serving the needs of scientific communities around the world.

20. Research and education institutions should take account of the new information and communication technologies, assess their impact and promote their use, for example through the development of electronic publishing and the establishment of virtual research and teaching environments or digital libraries. Science curricula should be adapted to take into account the impact of these new technologies on scientific work. The establishment of an international programme on Internet-enabled science and vocational education and teaching, alongside the conventional system,

should be considered in order to redress the limitations of educational infrastructure and to bring high-quality science education to remote locations.

21. The research community should be involved in regular discussion with the publishing, library and information technology communities to ensure that the authenticity and integrity of scientific literature are not lost with the evolution of the electronic information system. The dissemination and sharing of scientific knowledge are an essential part of the research process, and governments and funding agencies should therefore ensure that relevant infrastructure and other costs are adequately covered in research budgets. Appropriate legal frameworks are necessary as well.

2. Science for peace and development

22. Today, more than ever, the natural and social sciences and their applications are indispensable to development. Worldwide cooperation among scientists is a valuable and constructive contribution to global security and to the development of peaceful interactions among different nations, societies and cultures.

Science for basic human needs

23. Research specifically aimed at addressing the basic needs of the population should be a permanent chapter in every country's development agenda. In defining research priorities, the developing countreis and countries in transition should consider not only their needs and weaknesses in terms of scientific

capacity and information, but also their own strengths in terms of local knowledge, know-how and human and natural resources.

24. For a coutnry to have the capacity to provide for the basic needs of its population, science and technology education is a strategic necessity. As part of this education, students should learn to solve specific problems and to address the needs of society by utilizing scientific and technological knowlege and skills.

25. Industrialized countries should cooperate with developing countries through jointly defined S & T projects that respond to the basic problems of the population in the latter. Careful impact studies should be conducted to ensure better planning and implementation of development projects. Personnel engaged in such projects should receive training of relevance to their work.

26. All countires should share scientific knowledge and cooperate to reduce avoidable ill-health throughout the world. Each country should assess and so identify the health improvement prorities that are best suited to their own circumstances. National and regional research programmes aimed at reducing variations in health among communities, such as collecting good epidemiological and other statistical data and communicating corresponding best practice to those who can use it, should be introduced.

27. Innovative and cost-effective mechanisms for funding science and polling the S & T resources and efforts of different nations should be examined with a view

to their implementation by relevant institutions at the regional and international levels. Networks for human resources interchange, both North-South and South-South, should be set up. These networks should be so designed as to encourage scientists to use their expertise for the benefit of their own countries.

28. Donor countries, non-governmental and inter-governmental organizations and United Nations agencies should strengthen their programmes involving science to address pressing developmental problems as indicated in this *Science Agenda* while maintaining high quality standards.

Science, enviornment and sustainable development

29. National, regional and global environmental research programmes should be strengthened or developed, as appropriate, by governments, concerned United Nations agencies, the scientific community and private and public research funding institutions. These research programmes should include programmes for capacity building. Areas requiring special attention include the freshwater issue and the hydrological cycle, climate variations and change, oceans, coastal areas, polar regions, biodiversity, desertification, deforestation, biogeochemical cycles and natural hazards. The goals of the existing international global environmental research programmes should be vigorously pursued within the framework of Agenda 21 and the action plans of the global conferences. Cooperation between neighbouring countries or among countries having similar ecological conditions must be supported in the solution of common environmental problems.

30. All components of the earth system must be monitored systematically on a long-term basis; this requires enhanced support by governments and the private sector for the further development of the global environmental observing systems. The effectiveness of monitoring programmes depends crucially on the wide availability of monitored data.

31. Interdisciplinary research involving both the natural and the social sciences must be vigorously enhanced by all major actors concerned, including the private sector, to address the human dimension of global enviornmental change, including health impacts, and to improve understanding of sustainability as conditioned by natural systems. Insights into the concept of sustainable consumption also demand the interaction of natural sciences with social and political scientists, economists and demographers.

32. Modern scientific knowledge and traditional knowledge should be brought closer together in interdisciplinary projects dealing with the links between culture, environment and development in such areas as the conservation of biological diversity, management of natural resources, understanding of natural hazards and mitigation of their impact. Local communities and other relevant players should be involved in these projects. Individual scientists and the scientific community have a responsibility to communicate in clear language the scientific explanations of these issues and the ways in which science can play a key role in addressing them.

33. Governments, in co-operaiton with universities and higher education institutions, and with the help of

relevant United Nations organizations, should extend and improve education, training and facilities for human resources development in environment-related sciences, also utilizing traditional and local knowledge. Special efforts in this respect are required in developing countries, with the cooperation of the international community.

34. All countries should emphasize capacity-building in vulnerability and risk assessment, early warning of both short-lived natural disasters and long-term hazards of environmental change, improved preparedness, adaptation, mitigation of their effects and integration of disaster management into national development planning. It is important, however, to bear in mind that we live in a complex world with an inherent uncertainty about long-term trends. Decision-makers must take this into account and therefore encourage the development of new forecasting and monitoring strategies. The pre-cautionary principle is an important guiding principle in handling inevitable scientific uncertainty, especially in situations of potentially irreversible or catastrophic impacts.

35. S & T research on clean and sustainable technologies, recycling, renewable energy resources and efficient use of energy should be strongly supported by the public and private sectors at national and international levels. Competent international organizations, including UNESCO and the United Nations Industrial Development Organization (UNIDO), should promote the establishment of a freely accessible virtual library on sustainable technologies.

Science and technology

36. National authories and the private sector should shpport university-industry partnerships also involving research institutes and medium, small and micro enterprises, for promoting innovation, accelerating returns from science and generating benefits for all the participants.

37. Curricula relating to science and technology should encourage a scientific approach to problem-solving. University-industry cooperation should be promoted to assist engineering education and continuing vocational education and to enhance responsiveness to the needs of industry and support from industry to the education sector.

38. Countries should adopt best practices for advancing innovation, in a manner best suited to their needs and resources. Innovation is no longer a linear process arising from a single advance in science; it requires a systems approach involving partnerships, linkages between many areas of knowledge and constant feedback between many players. Possible initiatives include cooperative research centres and research networks, technology 'incubators' and research parks, and transfer and advisory bodies for small and medium enterprises. Specific policy instruments, including initiatives to encourage national innovation systems to address science technology links, should be developed taking tnto account global economic and technological changes. Science policy should promote the incorporation of knowledge into social and productive activities. It is imperative to tackle the

issue of the endogenous generation of technologies starting from problems faced by developing countries. This implies that these countries should have resources available to become generators of technologies.

39. Acceleration of technology transfer to promote industrial, economic and social development should be supported through the mobility of professionals between universities and industry and between countries, as well as through research networks and inter-firm partnerships.

40. Greater emphasis should be placed by governments and institutions of higher learning on engineering, technological and vocational education, also in the form of lifelong learning and through the means of international cooperation. New curriculum profiles which are consistent with the requirements of employers and attractive to youth should be defined. In order to mitigate the adverse impact of asymmetric migration of trained personnel from the developing to the developed countries and also to sustain high-quality education and research in developing countries, UNESCO could catalyse more symmetric and closer interaction of S & T personnel across the world and the establishment of world-class education and research infrastructure in the developing countries.

Science education

41. Governments should accord the highest priority to improving science education at all levels, with particular attention to the elimination of the effects of gender bias and bias against disadvantaged groups,

raising public awareness of science and fostering its popularization. Steps need to be taken to promote the professional development of teachers and educators in the face of change and special efforts should be made to address the lack of appropriately trained science teachers and educators, in particular in developing countries.

42. Science teachers at all levels and personnel involved in formal science education should have access to continuous updating of their knowledge for the best possible performance of their educational tasks.

43. New curricula, teaching methodologies and resources taking into account gender and cultural diversity should be developed by national education systems in response to the changing educational needs of societies. Research in science and technology education needs to be furthered nationally and internationally through the establishment and networking of specialized centres around the world, with the cooperation of UNESCO and other relevant international organizations.

44. Educational institutions should encourage the contribution of students to decision-making concerning education and research.

45. Governments should provide increased support to regional and international programmes of higher education and to networking of graduate and postgraduate institutions, with special emphasis on North-South and South-South cooperation, since they are important means of helping all countries, especially

the smaller or least developed among them, to strengthen their scientific and technological resource base.

46. Non-governmental organizations should play an important role in the sharing of experience in science teaching and education.

47. Educational institutions should provide basic science education to students in areas other than science. They should also provide opportunities for lifelong learning in the sciences.

48. Governments, international organizations and relevant professional institutions should enhance or develop programmes for the training of scientific journalists, communicators and all those involved in increasing public awareness of science. An international programme on promotion of scientific literacy and culture accessible to all should be considered in order to rpovide appropriate technology and scientific inputs in an easily understandable form that are conducive to the development of local communities.

49. National authorities and funding institutions should promote the role of science museums and centres as important elements in public education in science. Recognizing the resource constraints of developing countries, distance education should be used extensively to complement existing formal and non-formal education.

Science for peace and conflict resolution

50. The basic princiles of peace and coexistence should

be a part of education at all levels. Science students should also be made aware of their specific responsibility not to apply scientific knowledge and skills to activitieis which threaten peace and security.

51. Governmental and private funding bodies should strengthen or develop research institutions that carry out interdisciplinary researrch in the areas of peace and the peaceful applications of S &T. Each country should ensure its involvement in this work, whether at the national level or through participation in international activities. Public and private support for research on the causes and consequences of wars, and conflict prevention and resolution should be increased.

52. Governments and the private sector should invest in sectors of science and technology directly addressing issues that are at the root of potential conflicts, such as energy use, competition for resources, and pollution of air, soil and water.

53. Military and civil sectors, including scientists and engineers, should collaborate in seeking solutions to problems caused by accumulated weapon stocks and landmines.

54. A dialogue should be promtoed between representatives of governments, civil society and scientists in order to reduce millitary spending and the orientation of science towards military applications.

Science and policy

55. National policies should be adopted that imply consistent and long-term support for S &T, in order

to ensur the strengthening of the human resource base, establishment of scientific institutions, improvement and upgrading of science education, integration of science into the national culture, development of infrastructures and promotion of technology and innovation capacities.

56. S &T policies should be implemented that explicitly consider social relevance, peace, cultural diversity and gender differences. Adequate participatory mechanisms should be instituted to facilitate democratic debate on science policy choices. Women should actively particpate in the design of these policies.

57. All countries should systematically undertake analyses and studies on science and technology policy, taking into account the opinions of all relevant sectors of society, including those of young people, to define short-term and long-term strategies leading to sound and equitable socio-economic development. A World Technology Report as a companion volume to the present UNESCO *World Science Report* should be considered in order to provide a balanced world opinion on the impact of technology on social systems and culture.

58. Governments should support graduate programmes on S & T policy and social aspects of science. Training in legal and ethical issues and regulations guiding international R & D in strategic areas such as information and communication technologies, biodiversity and biotechnology should be developed for scientists and professionals concerned. Science mangers

and decision-makers should have regular access to training and updating to cope with the changing needs of modern society in the areas of S &T.

59. Governments should promote the further development or setting up of national statistical services capable of providing sound data, disaggregated by gender and disadvantaged groups, on science education and R & D activities that are necessary for effective S & T policy-making. Developing countries should be assisted in this respect by the international community, using the technical expertise of UNESCO and other international organizations.

60. Governments of developing countries and countries in transition should enhance the status of scientfiic, educational and technical careers, and make determined efforts to improve working conditions, increase their capacity to retain trained scientists and promote new careers in S & T areas. Programmes should also be set up or promoted to establish eollaboration with scientists, engineers and technologists who have emigrated from these countries to developed countries.

61. Governments should make an effort to use scientific expertise more systematically in policy-making addressing the process of economic and technological transformation. The contribution of scientists should be an integral part of programmes supporting either innovataion or measures aimed at industrial development or restructuring.

62. Scientific advice is an increasingly necessary factor for

informed policy-making in a complex world. Therefore, scientists and scientific bodies should consider it an important responsibility to provide independent advice to the best of their knowledge.

63. All levels of government should establish and regularly review mechanisms which ensure timely access to the best available advice from the scientific ommunity drawing on a sufficiently wide range of the best expert sources. These mechanisms should be open, objective and transparent. Governments should publish this scientific advice in media accessible to the public at large.

64. Governments, in cooperation with the agencies of the United Nations system and international scientific organizations, should strengthen international scientific advisorty processes as a necessary contribution to intergovernmental policy consensus-building at regional and global levels and to the implementation of regional and international conventions.

65. All countries should protect intellectual property rights, while recognizing that access to data and information is essential for scientific progress. In developing an appropriate international legal framework, World Intellectual Property Organization (WIPO), in cooperation with relevant international organizations, should constantly address the question of knoweldge monopolies, and the World Trade Organization (WTO), during new negotations of the Agreement on Trade-Related Aspects of Intellectual Property Rights (TRIPS), should incorporate into this

Agreement tools aimed at financing the advancement of science in the South with the full involvement of the scientific community. In this regard, the international programmes of ICSU and the five intergovernmental scientific programmes of UNESCO should play a catalytic role by, *inter alia,* improving the compatibility of data collection and processing, and facilitating access to scientific knowlege.

3. Science in society and Science for society

66. The practice of scientific research and the use of scientific knowledge should always aim at the welfare of humankind, be respectful of the dignity of human beings and of their fundamental rights, and take fully into account our shared responsibility towards future generations.

Social requirements and human dignity

67. Governments, international organizations and research institutions should foster interdisciplinary research aimed specifically at identifying, understanding and solving pressing human or social problems, according to each country's priorities.

68. All countries should encourage and support social science research to better understand and manage the tensions characterizing the relations between science and technology on the one hand, and the different societies and their institutions on the other hand. Transfer of technology should be accompanied by analysis of its possible impact on populations and society.

69. The structure of educational institutions and the design of their curricula should be made open and flexible so as to adjust to the emerging needs of societies. Young scientists should be provided with a knowledge and an understanding of social issues, and a capacity to move outside their specific field of specialization.

70. University curricula for science students should include field work that relates their studies to social needs and realities.

Ethical issues

71. The ethics and responsibility of science should be an integral part of the education and training of all scientists. It is important to instil in students a positive attitude towards reflection, alertness and awareness of the ethical dilemmas they may encounter in their professional life. Young scientists should be appropriately encouraged to respect an dadhere to the basic ethical principles and responsibilities of science. UNESCO's World Commission on the Ethics of Scientific Knowledge and Technology (COMEST), in cooperation with ICSU's Standing Committee on Responsibility and Ethics of Sciences (SCRES), have a special responsibility to follow up on this issue.

72. Research institutions should foster the study of ethical aspects of scientific work. Special interdisciplinary research programmes are needed to analyse and monitor the ethical implications and means of regulation of scientific work.

73. The international scientific community, in cooperation with other actors, should foster a debate, including a public debate, promtoing enviornmental ethics and environmental codes of conduct.

74. Scientific insitutions are urged to comply with ethical norms, and to respect the freedom of scientists to express themselves on ethical issues and to denounce misuse or abuse of scientific or technological advances.

75. Governments and non-governmental organizations, in particular scientific and scholarly organizations, should organize debates, including public debates, on the ethical implicatios of scientific work. Scientists and scientific and scholarly organizations should be adequately represented in the relevant regulating and decision-making bodies. These activities should be institutionally fostered and recognized as part of scientists' work and responsibility. Scientific associations should define a code of ethics for their members.

76. Governments should encourage the setting up of adequate mechanisms to address ethical issues concerning the use of scientific knowledge and its applications, and such mechanisms should be established where they do not yet exist. Non-governmental organizations and scientific institutions should promote the establishment of ethics committees in their field of competence.

77. Member States of UNESCO are urged to strengthen the activities of the International Bioethics committee and of the World Commission on the Ethics of

Scientific Knowledge and Technology and ensure appropriate representation.

Widening participation in science

78. Government agencies, international organizations and universities and research institutions should ensure the full participation of women in the planning, orientation, conduct and assessment of research activities. It is necessary that women participate actively in shaping the agenda for the future direction of scientific research.

79. The full participation of disadvantaged groups in all aspects of research activities, including the development of policy, also needs to be ensured.

80. All countries should contribute to the collection of reliable data, in an internationally standardized manner, for the generation of gender-disaggregated statistics on S & T, in cooperation with UNESCO and other relevant international organizations.

81. Governments and educational institutions should identify and eliminate, from the early learning stages on, educational practices that have a discriminatory effect, so as to increase the successful participation in science of individuals from all sectors of society, including disadvantaged groups.

82. Every effort should be made to eliminate open or covert discriminatory practices in research activitieis. More flexible and permeable structures should be set up to facilitate the access of young scientists to careers in science. Measures aimed at attaining social equity

in all scientific and technological activities, including working conditions, should be designed, implemented and monitored.

Modern science and other systems of knowledge

83. Governments are called upon to formulate national policies that allow a wider use of the applications of traditional forms of learning and knowledge, while at the same time ensuring that its commercialization is properly rewarded.
84. Enhanced support for activities at the national and international levels on traditional and local knowledge systems should be considered.
85. Countries should promote better understanding and use of traditional knowledge systems, instead of focusing only on extracting elements for their perceived utility to the S & T system. Knowledge should flow simultaneously to and from rural communities.
86. Governmental and non-governmental organizations should sustain traditional knowledge systems through active support to the societies that are keepers and developers of this knowledge, their ways of life, their languages, their social organization and the environments in which they live, and fully recognize the contribution of women as repositories of a large part of traditional knowledge.
87. Governments should support cooperation between holders of traditional knowledge and scientists to explore the relationships between different knowledge systems and to foster interlinkages of mutual benefit.

FOLLOW-UP

88. We, participants in the World Conference on Science, are prepared to act with determination to attain the goals proclaimed in the *Declaration on Science and the Use of Scientific Knowledge,* and uphold the recommendations for follow-up set out hereafter.

89. All participants in the Conference consider the *Agenda* as a framework for action, and encourage other partners to adhere to it. In so doing, governments, the United Nations system and all other stakeholders should use the *Agenda,* or relevant parts of it, when planning and implementing concrete measures and activities which embrace science or its applications. In this way, a truly multilateral and multifaceted programme of action will be developed and carried out. We are also convinced that young scientists should play an important role in the follow-up of this *Framework for Action.*

90. Taking into account the outcome of the six regional forums on women and science sponsored by UNESCO, the Conference stresses that special efforts should be made by governments, educational institutions, scientific communities, non-governmental organizations and civil society, with support from bilateral and international agencies, to ensure the full participation of women and girls in all aspects of science and technology, and to this effect to:

- promote within the education system the access of girls and women to scientific education at all levels;

- improve conditions for recruitment, retention and advancement in all fields of research;
- launch, in collaboration with UNESCO and the United Nations Development Fund for Women (UNIFEM), national, regional and global campaigns to raise awareness of the contribution of women to science and technology, in order to overcome existing gender stereotypes among scientists, policy-makers and the community at large;
- undertake research, supported by the collection and analysis of gender-disaggregated data, documenting constraints and progress in expanding the role of women in science and technology;
- monitor the implementation of and document best practices and lessons learned through impact assessment and evaluations;
- ensure an appropriate representation of women in national, regional and international policy- and decision-making bodies and forums;
- establish an international network of women scientists;
- continue to document the contributions of women in science and technology.

To sustain these initiatives governments should create appropriate mechanisms, where these do not yet exist, to propose and monitor introduction of the necessary policy changes in support of the attainment of these goals.

91. Special efforts also need to be made to ensure the full participation of disadvantaged groups in science and technology, and they should include:

- removing barriers in the education system;
- removing barriers in the research system;
- raising awareness of the contribution of these groups to science and technology in order to overcome existing stereotypes;
- undertaking research, supported by the collection of data, documenting constraints;
- monitoring implementation of and documenting best practices;
- ensuring representation in policy-making bodies and forums.

92. Although the follow-up to the Conference will be executed by many partners who will retain the responsibility for their own action, UNESCO, in co-operation with ICSU - its partner in convening the Conference - should act as a clearing house. For this purpose, all the partners should send UNESCO information about their follow-up initiatives and action. In this context, UNESCO and ICSU should develop concrete initiatives for international scientific cooperation together with relevant United Nations organizations and bilateral donors, in particular on a regional basis.

93. UNESCO and ICSU should submit the *Declaration on Science and the Use of Scientific Knowledge and Science Agenda-Framework for Action* to their General

Conference and General Assembly respectively, with a view to enabling both organizations to identify and envisage follow-up action in their respective programmes and provide enhanced support for that purpose. The other partner organizations should do likewise vis-a-vis their governing bodies; the United Nations General Assembly should also be seized of the outcome of the World Conference on Science.

94. The international community should support the efforts of developing countries in implementing this *Science Agenda*.

95. The Director-General of UNESCO and the President of ICSU should ensure that the outcome of the Conference is disseminated as widely as possible, which includes transmitting the *Declaration* and the *Science Agenda - Framework for Action* to all countries, to relevant international and regional organizations and to multilateral institutions. All participants are encouraged to contribute to such dissemination.

96. We appeal for increased partnership between all the stakeholders in science and recommend that UNESCO, in cooperation with other partners, prepare and conduct a regular review of the follow-up to the World Conference on Science. In particular, no later than 2001, UNESCO and ICSU shall prepare jointly an analytical report to governments and international partners on the returns on the Conference, the execution of follow-up and further action to be taken.

4

Principles and commitments contained in the documents of the World Conference on Science

Basis For Follow-Up Activities

In adopting the Declaration and the *Science Agenda-*framework for Action after substantial revision by all participants, the Budapest Conference established a basis for the alliance between science and society for the coming century, and defined guidelines to orient the action of the different parterns involved. A summary of the basic principles and commitments contained in these documents is presented below as a practical guide. The conference participants have committed themselves to these principles and actions, and UNESCO and ICSU will actively promote their implementation.

Main principles contained in the *Declaration*

- There is an urgent need to use scientific knowledge from all fields in a responsible manner to address human needs and aspirations. The practice and use of science should always aim at the welfare of humankind, present and future.

- Fundamental and problem-oriented research are essential for achieving endogenous development.

- Appropriate education and research programmes in S & T, especially in developing countries, need sustained support from governments and the private sector.

- Science education at all levels and without discrimination is a fundamental requisite for democracy. Equality in access to science is not only a social and ethical requirement: it is a necessity for realizing the full human intellectual potential.

- Expanded science literacy, ability and skills, and an appreciation of ethical values, are needed to improve public decision-making on science issues.

- Enhanced regional and international cooperation are needed to support scientific capacity building, especially in the small states and the least developed countries.

- New initiatives are required for interdisciplinary collaboration and for co-operation between different sectors involved in the production and use of scientific knowledge. The objective should be a move towards sustainable development strategies through integration of economic, social, cultural and environmental dimensions.

- Use of information and communication technologies for free flow of knowledge should be expanded, with due respect for the diversity of cultures and plurality of expression.

- Intellectual property rights need to be protected on a global basis. Legal frameworks should meet the specific requirements of developing countries and traditional knowledge, its sources and products.

Main commitments and activities contained in the Science Agenda (numbers refer to paragraphs)

Commitment to support or promote:	by governments	by universities and research institutions	by scientists and the scientific community	by the private sector and funding agencies	by NGOs and society at large
1	2	3	4	5	6
research and new ways of funding it	7,14,15	10		15,16	
research and teaching related to social needs	23,26,52,67	67,69,70		52	
research to solve environmental problems	29,30,35	29	29	29,30,35	
interdisciplinary research and education	67	10,31,67	31	31	
research on the impact of technology on society	57,61,68				
science education	24,41,42,43,45	9,10,11,20,42,43,44,47	9		46
engineering education	24,40	40			
science communication and popularization	48,49	10,48		49	48
participation of women in science	41,43,78,80,81,90	17,43,78,81,82,90	17,90		90
involvement of students in decision-making		44			
environmental education and ethics	33	33	73		

(Contd...)

1	2	3	4	5	6
capacity building in disaster mitigation	34				
university-industry partnerships	36, 38, 39	16,37,38,39	61	16,36,38,39	
ethics of science	8, 75, 76, 77	50, 71, 72, 74	13, 50, 71, 75		75, 76
science for peaceful purposes	51, 52, 53, 54		53, 54	51, 52	53,54
science for development	23, 28		28		
science and technology policies	8, 38, 55, 56, 57, 58, 59	58			
scientific advice for policy makers and public sector	61, 63, 64		62, 64		
national research systems in developing countries	12, 60			12	
international co-operation	7, 26, 27, 29, 45	9, 11, 17, 27	9, 13, 17, 27	27	
scientific collaboration with developing countries	12, 18, 19, 25				
knowledge sharing and access to scientific information	15, 18	9,17	9,17		
scientific publishing; electronic publishing	19. 21	20, 21		21	
protection of intellectual property rights	8, 65		65		
understanding and use of traditional knowledge	33, 83, 84, 85, 86, 87	33	32		32, 85, 86
participation of disadvantaged groups	41, 81, 91	17, 79, 81, 82, 91	17, 91		91

NOTE

Subsequent to the World Conference on Science, both *Declaration and Framework* documents were fully endorsed by the governing bodies of ICSU and UNESCO: the 26th General Assembly of ICSU, meeting in Cairo in September 1999, and the 30th Session of the UNESCO General Conference, convened in Paris, October/November 1999.

In endorsing both Declaration and *Framework,* the ICSU General Assembly expressed concern over the use of the phrase 'traditional and local knowledge systems' in the texts.

It acknowledged the importance of empirical knowledge built up over generations and grounded in practical evidence, but considered that such knowledge had to be distinguished from approaches that seek to promote anti-science and pseudo-science, and that degrade the values of science as understood by the ICSU community.

The Assembly reaffirmed its support for the values and methods of verifiable science. It recognized the relation between traditional knowledge and modern science to be both important and a highly complex political and sociological question and requested the Executive Board of ICSU to set up a critical study on the issue.

At the subsequent 30th Session of the UNESCO General Conference, representatives of Member States expressed agreement with this view, and requested UNESCO to associate itself with such a study.

NOTE

Subsequent to the World Conference on Science, both Declaration and Framework documents were fully endorsed by the governing bodies of ICSU and UNESCO: the 26th General Assembly of ICSU meeting at Cairo in September 1999, and the 30th Session of the UNESCO General Conference, convened in Paris, October/November 1999.

In endorsing both Declaration and Framework, the ICSU General Assembly expressed concern over the use of the phrase 'traditional and local knowledge systems' in the texts.

It acknowledged the importance of empirical knowledge built up over generations and grounded in practical evidence but considered that such knowledge had to be distinguished from approaches that seek to promote anti-science and pseudo-science, and that degrade the values of science as understood by the ICSU community.

The Assembly reaffirmed its support for the values and methods of verifiable science; it recognized the relation between traditional knowledge and modern science to be both important and a highly complex political and sociological question and requested the Executive Board of ICSU to set up a critical study on the issue.

At the subsequent 30th Session of the UNESCO General Conference, representatives of Member States expressed agreement with this view and requested UNESCO to associate itself with such a study.